# FACT FINDERS

## Educational adviser: Arthur Razzell

# North American Indians

Robin May

Illustrated by Dick Eastland  Richard Hook  John Sibbick
Annette Wade
Designed by Faulkner/Marks Partnership

Macmillan Education Limited

916

# North American Indians

# A Land of Many Nations

**Eskimo (1)**

**Tlingit (2)**

The first Indians came to America from Asia about 30,000 years ago. They headed south and settled in different parts, as the map shows.

This book is about the Indians who settled in what became the United States of America.

①

②

⑧ ⑦

⑨

**Navaho (9)**

**Blackfoot (8)**

**Cree (3)**

**Ojibwa (4)**

③
④

The explorer Columbus gave the Indians their name. When he arrived in America, he thought he had reached India.

The early European settlers called the Indians 'red' because their light brown skins looked red in sunny weather.

**Mandan (7)**

⑥
⑤

**Creek (5)**

**Cherokee (6)**

# Indian Homes

In the east, the Indians lived in small groups of huts (below). The Iroquois huts were 30 metres long and were called longhouses.

Many other Indians had dome-shaped huts called wigwams, made of wood and bark.

Some Indians, like the Mandans, lived in earth lodges (below right).

**Haida house**

**Earth lodge**

**Tepee**

Tepees, or tipis, were another kind of Indian home. The Blackfoot Indians lived in tepees (above).

In the far north-west beside the Pacific Ocean, the Indians built solid houses from wooden planks. Some were covered with carvings, like the Haida house above.

# On the Move

The Spanish brought horses when they came to America nearly 500 years ago. Until then, the Indians travelled on foot. Braves (warriors) could jog through woods and across prairies for hours and they would still be able to fight (below).

Indians who lived by rivers and lakes travelled by canoe (right).

**Iroquois braves**

Chippewa canoe

Cheyennes on horseback

Cheyennes travelling

Some Indians carried their belongings on the poles from their tepees (left). Before horses came, dogs dragged the poles.

All the tribes had horses by about 200 years ago. The Indians became very good riders, like the Cheyennes above.

# The Buffalo Hunt

The Indians of the west could not live without the buffalo, or bison. They used its flesh for food, and other parts were used in their homes and clothing. Horseshoes, shields, cups and many other things the Indians needed were all made from the buffalo (below).

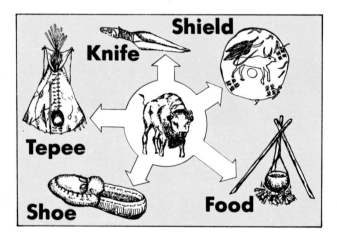

**Shield**

**Knife**

**Tepee**

**Shoe**

**Food**

The Indians hunted the buffalo for sport as well as to kill the animal. At first, they hunted on foot, but later they hunted on horseback (right).

There were many millions of buffalo until the white men came and killed almost all of them. The white men wanted their skins for coats.

The white men also knew how much the Indians needed the buffalo. They knew that the Indians would have no food without the buffalo, and then they could beat the Indians more easily.

# Women and Children

Pocahontas was a famous Indian woman who had a very unusual life (left). She married an English settler and visited London. She wore English clothes to meet King James I.

Other Indian women had more ordinary lives. In the east, the squaws (wives) helped to govern their tribes.

**(Above) Pocahontas**

**Navaho grinding corn**

**Choctaw weaver**

**Tewa potter**

In the west, the women had to do all the hard work on the buffalo. They had to turn the animals into food and clothing

In all the tribes, women were not as important as men, but each Indian family lived happily together. Indian parents often spoiled their children.

# What They Wore

Indians usually went into battle with bare chests, but the clothes they did wear were often very beautiful.

Indian clothes were made from the skins of animals like buffalo and deer. Their soft shoes were called moccasins.

**Kwa-kiutl chief** **from north-west coast**

**Iowa chief from mid-west prairies**

Indian men wore more beautiful clothes than Indian women, and the Indians in each area had their own way of dressing.

The best known Indian clothing belongs to the Sioux and Cheyennes. They lived on the Great Plains of America.

**Nez Percé woman from north-west**

**Apache chief from south-west**

# Medicine

The Indians worshipped the sun and the earth. They believed in 'medicine' which means magic power. The Indians had 'medicine men' who were their doctors, priests and fortune tellers. The medicine men wore masks to protect themselves from evil spirits (below).

Many Indians tortured themselves for religious reasons (left). They did not feel pain because they were in a trance.

Before hunting, they sometimes danced a buffalo dance to bring them luck in the hunt (above). Before battles, they danced war dances.

# Indian Weapons

Before the white men came, Indians did not know how to use metal. They made their bows, arrows and clubs from stone, wood and bone. They made their shields from buffalo skin.

Then the first white men came, and the Indians began to get hold of their guns. They learned to use the metal from them.

**Axe with stone blade**

**Flint for war club**

**Spearhead**

**War clubs**

**Early Indian with weapons**

**Spear with metal blade**

The Indians started to use
etal.
   Soon, they had metal knives
nd steel axes and they
pped their arrows with metal.
   But then the white men began
 make rifles that could shoot
 st. These were much better
 an the Indian weapons.

**Shield**

**Pipe
toma-
hawk
(pipe
and
axe
in
one)**

**Quiver with
bow and arrows**

**Metal
knife**

**Later
Indian
with rifle**

# The Indian Wars

There were only about a million Indians in America when the white men came. The white men soon wanted the Indians's land so they fought the Indians and pushed them further and further west.

Sometimes, the white men used Indian scouts like the one on the right to track down other Indians.

**(Above) Indian Scout**

**French explorer**

**Iroquois**

Some tribes were still fighting about 90 years ago. But there were too many white people and there were railways to bring white soldiers. The Indians did not have enough weapons, and the buffalo were gone. The Indians had to surrender in the end.

**Cheyenne**

# Glossary

**Apaches**   Fierce Indians who lived in the deserts and mountains of the south-west.

**Bison**   The real name for the American buffalo.

**Brave**   The name for an Indian warrior.

**Buffalo dance**   A dance which Indians danced before a hunt to make the hunt successful.

**Cheyennes**   One of the tribes of Plains Indians.

**Earth lodge**   An Indian hut built of mud.

**Longhouse**   The long hut of the Iroquois.

**Indian scout**   An Indian used as a guide by white men. White men also used scouts to track down wanted Indians.

**Moccasins**   Indian shoes made of soft animal skins.

**Plains Indians**   The tribes who lived on the Great Plains of America, between the Missouri River and the Rocky Mountains.

**Prairies**   Grasslands.

**Sioux**   One of the most famous tribes of Plains Indians.

**Squaw**   A white man's name for an Indian's wife.

**Tepee**   An Indian home made of a ring of wooden poles tied together at the top and covered with skins.

**Wigwam**   A round Indian hut made of wood and covered with bark.

**Photo Credits:** British Museum, Werner Forman Archive, Mansell Collection, Robin May, National Portrait Gallery, Smithsonian Institution

1 2 3 4 5 6 7 8 9 10— R  —85 84 83 82 81 80